Making the Modern World
Europe

West Europe

D. B. O'Callaghan

Longman

Europe in ruins, 1945

British troops in the ruins of a German town

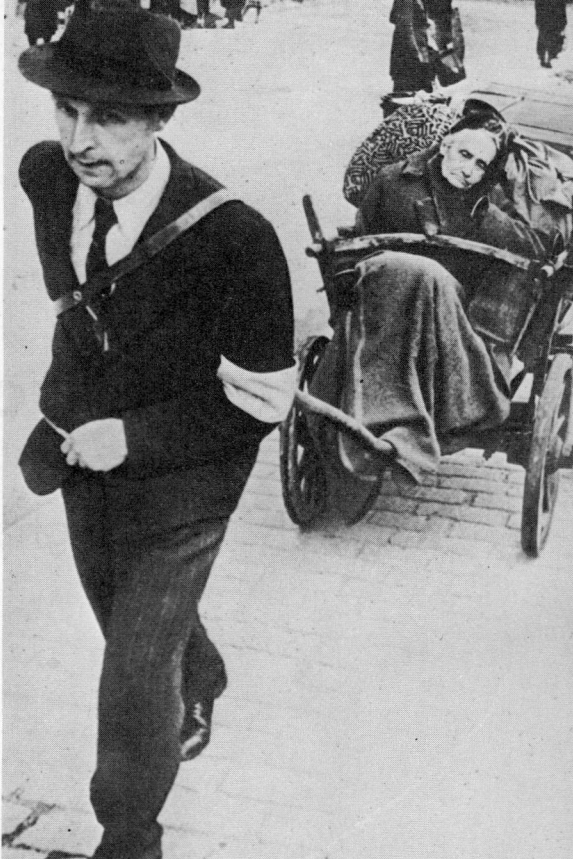

German refugees flee as the armies advance

Germany, 1945. Fighter aircraft scream low over roads packed with fleeing refugees. Tanks rumble through the smoking ruins of towns and villages. In an underground shelter in Berlin hides the shaking wreck of a man. Russian soldiers are fighting their way street by street towards his hideout. As his capital city is pounded into rubble above his head, Germany's dictator,

Adolf Hitler, waits for the end.

It came towards the end of April. Deep in the heart of Germany British and American troops advancing from the west met Russian troops moving in from the east. A week later Hitler killed himself. In the days which followed the German armies everywhere laid down their arms. Bonfires were lit all over Europe and people danced in the streets

2

A wrecked bridge on the river Rhine

to celebrate the end of the most terrible war the world had ever known.

But when the rejoicing was over, people looked around them and began to count the cost. Millions were dead. Millions more were homeless. Thousands of refugees wandered the roads searching desperately for food and shelter. Around them Europe lay in ruins. Hundreds of cities, towns and villages were just piles of rubble. Bridges had been blown up, railway lines destroyed, millions of acres of farmland turned into desert. The destruction seemed almost endless.

This was the Europe to which an uneasy peace came in 1945. A continent of ruined cities, shattered industries and hungry people. This book tells what happened in the years that followed.

3

The Allies fall out

In the picture soldiers from Soviet Russia and the United States meet one another in the centre of Germany in 1945. Yet even before Germany was beaten there had been signs that this wartime friendship might not last.

Soviet Russia had suffered terribly from the Germans. Twenty million of her people had died. Her richest farm land and most modern cities had been ruined. The Russian leader, Stalin, was determined to make his country safe from any future attack. He decided that Russia must have a screen of friendly nations between her and Germany. This meant making sure that all Russia's neighbours had friendly governments — even if many of their people did not want such governments.

The American and British leaders agreed. But they were not happy about the arrangement. They didn't like communism, the system of government in Russia, and they didn't want it to spread to other countries. Churchill feared that Stalin might try to take Hitler's place as master of the whole of Europe.

President Truman, of the United States shared Churchill's fear. He met Stalin in 1945 and came away believing that the Russian leader was planning to conquer the world. He started thinking of ways to stop Russian power from spreading.

At first Truman hoped that Britain would be able to check Russian power in Europe. But the war had left Britain too weak. The United States had to

An American and a Russian soldier watch the defeated German army going home

After the war the leaders of the allies met at Potsdam. The picture shows Prime Minister Attlee, President Truman and Joseph Stalin

Europe divided by the Iron Curtain

take her place.

The first time this happened was in 1947 when Truman sent help to the government in Greece. This help prevented an army of Greek communists from winning a civil war. This idea of using American power to stop other countries from coming under Russian influence came to be called the Truman Doctrine.

Meanwhile Stalin strengthened his grip on east Europe. In the last months of the war the Russian armies drove the Germans out of east Europe and set up governments friendly to Soviet Russia. At first, Stalin let both communists and non-communists hold posts in them. But gradually all those who would not obey the Russians were driven out or put in prison. The United States and Britain protested but it made no difference. By 1948 most of east Europe was under the rule of communist governments who did what the Russians told them.

It was clear that a new kind of war had begun—a Cold War. There was no fighting but there was always distrust and quarrelling. Churchill had seen this coming. In a speech in 1946 he spoke of an Iron Curtain which had fallen across Europe. On one side were Soviet Russia and the communist countries of east Europe. On the other were the United States, Britain and the nations of west Europe.

Rebuilding Europe – The Marshall plan

George Marshall speaking at a meeting of the U.N.

In June 1947, a retired American general named George Marshall made a speech at an American university. Marshall was the Secretary of State in the American government. This meant that he was in charge of America's dealings with other countries.

The United States was the only country which World War Two had made better off. Her land had not been fought over. Her cities had not been bombed. She had built many new factories. During the war these factories had made aeroplanes, tanks and other weapons. Now they stood ready to do other work.

General Marshall offered the help of the United States to the nations of Europe. Up to 1947, Europe's recovery from World War Two had been painfully slow. Factories, farms and mines were producing far less than they had done before the war. Millions of people were still without work, without decent homes, without sufficient food. They were becoming desperate. There seemed a chance that they might turn to communism as a way out of their difficulties.

The United States did not want this to happen. She had all the things needed to put Europe back on its feet—food, fuel, machinery, raw materials. The trouble was, that Europe could not afford to buy them. To get round this problem Marshall offered to *give* the European countries the goods they

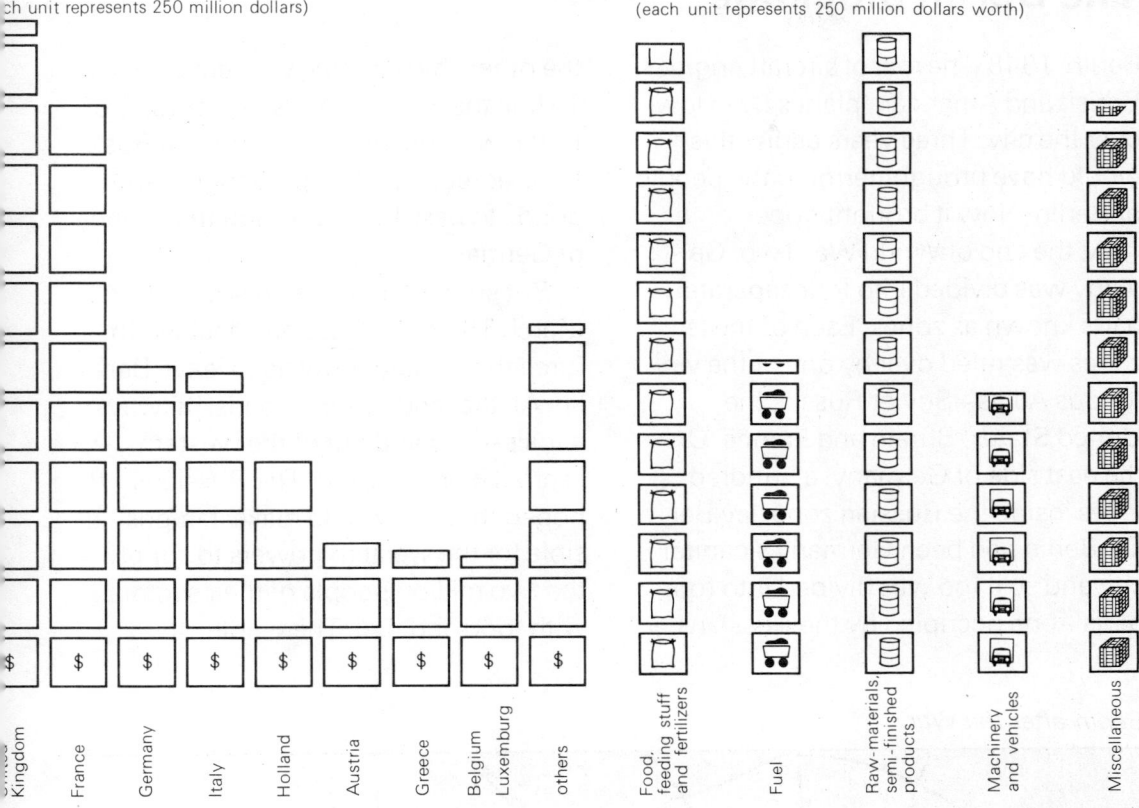

United Kingdom · France · Germany · Italy · Holland · Austria · Greece · Belgium Luxemburg · others

Food, feeding stuff and fertilizers · Fuel · Raw-materials, semi-finished products · Machinery and vehicles · Miscellaneous

were short of. He asked them to get together to decide what they needed so they could send the United States a kind of shopping list.

By July 1947, sixteen countries had accepted Marshall's invitation. Most of them jumped at the plan. 'When the Marshall proposals were announced, I grabbed them with both hands', said Ernest Bevin, Britain's Foreign Secretary.

The only people who didn't like this idea were the Russians. They thought that the Marshall plan was a plot to give the United States control of the industry and trade of Europe. They re-

fused to take part. They also made sure that none of the other countries on their side of the Iron Curtain took part.

But for the next five years American aid flooded into west Europe. The kind of goods that were sent, and the countries they went to, can be seen on the diagrams.

The Marshall plan brought food and shelter to millions of cold and hungry people. It got factories working again. It also showed the countries of Europe how they could benefit from working together. This was something they did not forget.

7

The Berlin blockade

Berlin, 1948. The roar of aircraft engines. British and American 'planes fly in low over the city. Three years earlier this would have brought terror to the people of Berlin. Now it brought hope.

At the end of World War Two, Germany was divided into four separate parts known as zones. Each of these zones was ruled over by one of the victorious Allies—Soviet Russia, the United States, Britain and France. On the east side of Germany, a hundred miles inside the Russian zone, lay Berlin. Berlin had been Germany's capital city and so it too was divided into four parts—one occupied by the Russians, the others by the three western powers. To link the western parts (or sectors) of Berlin with the outside world, the Russians agreed to allow passengers and goods to pass freely through their zone of Germany.

But soon there were quarrels. In March 1948, the Russians decided to force the western powers to leave Berlin. All the land routes—roads, railways, canals—into and out of the western sectors were blocked. The Russians hoped that this would make it impossible for the western powers to supply the two million people of their sectors with food and fuel. The whole city

Berlin after the War

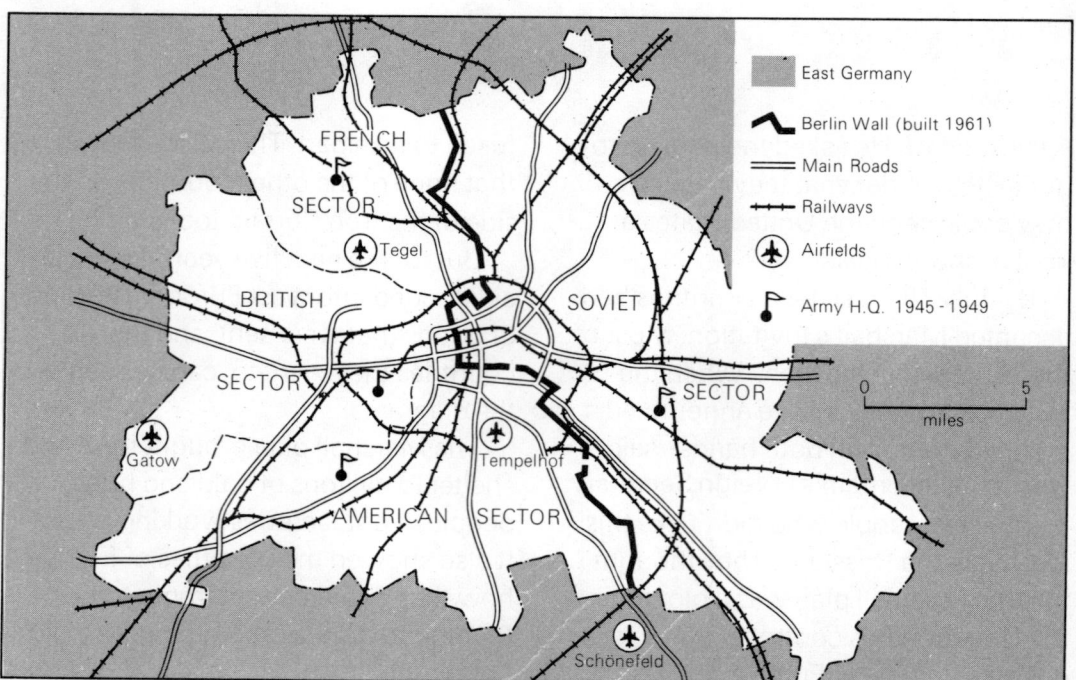

Berlin children cheer as an American 'plane flies in

would then pass under their control.

The western powers were determined not to let this happen. But to feed its people west Berlin needed hundreds of tons of food a day. To keep its factories going thousands of tons of other goods were needed. The western powers had two choices. The first was to send tanks to force a way through to Berlin by road. This would mean risking another war. So they chose the second way. They decided to keep west Berlin supplied by air.

In June 1948 the Berlin Airlift began.

It went on for almost a year. At one time heavily loaded transport 'planes were roaring in to land at a rate of one every 45 seconds, night and day. When the air fields became crowded, flying boats came skimming down onto the city's boating lakes. Altogether 280,000 flights were made and over 2,300,000 tons of food and supplies were flown in.

By May 1949, the Russians realised that their attempt to gain control of Berlin had failed. Stalin called off the blockade and the roads and railways into Berlin were opened.

The birth of west Germany

British tank in the Western Zone, 1950

When the war-time allies divided Germany the idea was that this would be only a temporary arrangement. One day they intended to unite the whole country under one government. But both the Russians and the western powers wanted to be sure that this re-united Germany would be ruled by a government which was friendly towards them. The Russians felt especially strongly about this. They had suffered more at the hands of the Germans than anyone. The only friendly Germany they could think of was a Germany under communist rule.

But most Germans feared and disliked the Russians. It was clear that they would never elect a communist government of their own free will. So the Russians decided to keep their zone of Germany separate from the rest. This way they could make sure that communists would rule at least the eastern part of Germany.

The Berlin blockade made the western powers give up hope of reaching agreement with the Russians about Germany's future. After all, if they couldn't agree how to run Berlin, what hope was there of reaching agreement about the whole of Germany? In 1949, they decided to unite their zones of Germany without bothering about the Russian zone.

First of all elections were held — the first in which the German people were free to vote as they wished for nearly 20 years. After the elections the western powers put their zones together to form the Federal German Republic (usually called West Germany). Its first Chancellor (a position roughly the same as the British Prime Minister) was Konrad Adenauer. He held this position until he retired in 1963 at the age of 87. Because of his great age the people of west Germany usually called Adenauer simply 'The Old Man'.

But although west Germany was allowed to choose its own rulers, their powers were limited. In 1949 people still remembered the horrible crimes of Hitler and his Nazi followers. Most leading Nazis had been imprisoned or executed but nobody was ready yet to trust any Germans very far. So West Germany was not allowed to have any soldiers of her own and was still occupied by the troops of the western powers.

Konrad Adenauer in 1956

Vote for the SPD (Socialist Party)

Germany's economic miracle

In 1945 Germany was a defeated and hungry nation. Her cities were in ruins. Millions of her people were living in cellars, in shacks and under railway arches. The ration of food was less than half of what is needed to keep anyone in good health. Yet within 15 years West Germany had become one of Europe's richest nations. Its people were among the best off in the world.

This 'economic miracle', as it is sometimes called, began at the end of the 1940's. One reason for it was the money and raw materials which flooded into Germany under the Marshall Plan. Another, oddly enough, was the bombing into ruins of Germany's factories during the war. When the war ended the Germans had to build up their industries from scratch. By the 1950's they had some of the most up-to-date factories and equipment in the world.

As early as 1951, the factories and mines of West Germany were already producing more goods than they had done before the war. Many of these goods were sold to other countries. German-made Volkswagen cars, for example, were seen on the roads of almost every country in the world. By 1961, West Germany was exporting more goods to other countries than the whole of Germany had done before the war.

Evidence of the economic miracle. Cologne in 1965

A gateway in the Berlin wall, looking east

The Berlin wall

The 'economic miracle' made the people of west Germany very prosperous. In east Germany (the part under Communist rule) the people were nowhere near so well off. Partly because of this, millions of east Germans fled to the west during the 1950's. Many of these escapers were skilled workers, whom east Germany could not afford to lose.

The favourite escape route was through West Berlin. All an east German had to do was to catch a tram from east to west Berlin and just not bother to come back. To block this route, in 1961 the government of east Germany built the Berlin Wall. You can see a section of the wall in the picture above. It is seven to thirteen feet high, twentyseven miles long and backed up by ditches, watch towers and a 100 yard wide forbidden zone which no-one is allowed to enter. Anyone who does so risks being shot down by guards like those in the picture.

NATO and German re-armament

It took over five years to beat the Germans in World War Two. Millions died. Thousands of homes and work places were blasted into rubble. When the fighting ended the victorious allies set out to make sure that the Germans would never again cause such misery and destruction. They all agreed that she must never again have an army or weapons of any kind.

But, by the end of the 1940's, the nations of west Europe were more afraid of the Soviet Union than of Germany. In 1949 they joined together with the United States to form the North Atlantic Treaty Organisation (NATO) to guard against a possible Russian attack. The idea was that if any member of NATO was attacked, all the others would help to defend it. Combined land, air and sea forces were set up. These were placed under the command of General Eisenhower who had led the armies of the western allies in the war

German generals surrender to Field marshal Montgomery, April 1945

against Hitler.

The Russians replied to these moves by organising the nations of East Europe into a military alliance of their own, called the Warsaw Pact.

At first the United States gave most of the men and weapons for NATO. But in the early 1950's she had large armies fighting the communists in Korea and it was difficult for her to find as many soldiers for NATO. Some people were afraid that this might tempt Russia and the Warsaw Pact countries to attack west Europe.

To get more soldiers the NATO countries decided to re-arm West Germany and make her a member of NATO. But West Germany could hardly be expected to provide soldiers for NATO while she was still being treated as a defeated enemy. So, in May 1955, the western powers recognised the Federal German Republic (West Germany) as a fully independent country.

The way West Germany's armed forces grew after that time is shown on the diagram. By the end of the 1960's her army was larger than Britain's.

Not everyone was happy about this. The Russians feared that a strong west Germany might one day attack east Germany, to bring all Germans under one government. Even some of west Germany's friends were a little uneasy about the growing strength of her armed forces. They became still more worried when a political party reminding people of Hitler's Nazis began to gain some support at the end of the 1960's.

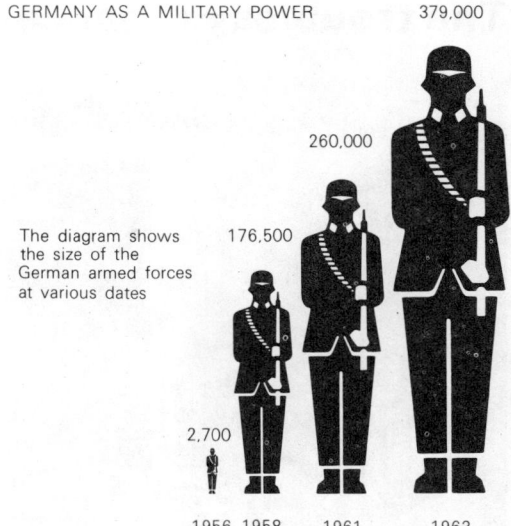

GERMANY AS A MILITARY POWER

379,000

260,000

176,500

The diagram shows the size of the German armed forces at various dates

2,700

1956 1958   1961   1963

Soldiers of the new German army training

The troubles of France's fourth republic

De Gaulle in Paris, August 1944

The picture above was taken in August 1944. It shows General Charles De Gaulle on perhaps the proudest day of his life. He is walking through Paris just after the liberation of the city from the Germans.

In 1940 France was conquered by the Germans. De Gaulle escaped to England. There he organised other Frenchmen into an army to continue the fight against the Germans. His men were called the Free French. They had their own uniforms and their own badge, the double cross of Lorraine.

By the end of the war most people looked upon De Gaulle as the leader of France. In 1945, he became the head of the country's government. But he soon became tired of the quarrelling between his countrymen and gave up the job. Not everyone was sorry to see him go. De Gaulle was a man who like to get his own way. Some people feared that if he stayed he might make himself into a dictator.

A new constitution or way of government was then set up in France. It was called the Fourth Republic. Its biggest weakness was that no government could stay in power long enough to make a really good job of tackling the country's problems. Yet in some ways France made progress. The war damage was gradually repaired. Factories were re-equipped with up-to-date machinery. Trade with other countries grew

French troops at the battle of Dien Bien Phu in Vietnam. After they lost this battle the French withdrew from the country

steadily. Perhaps most important of all, France played a leading part in persuading the countries of west Europe to work together more closely in matters of industry and trade.

But the Fourth Republic saw many failures. At home, no government could stop prices from rising. Abroad there were even more serious problems. France still had colonies—that is, foreign lands over which she ruled. The people of these colonies now wanted to rule themselves. In Indo-China (part of which is now called Vietnam) this led to a long war in which the French were defeated.

But France's biggest colonial problem was Algeria. Algeria is in North Africa. Most Frenchmen looked on it as part of France itself rather than as a colony. Many white people had settled there and set up farms and businesses.

But the native people of Algeria belonged to the Arab race. They disliked being part of France and wanted to rule themselves. In 1954, they began fighting the French for their freedom. It was a dirty, savage war which cost France a lot of money and the lives of many young men. Yet many Frenchmen felt that they had to fight on until the Algerians were beaten. To give up, they felt, would show everyone that France no longer counted as a great power. Many too had relatives or friends who had made their homes in Algeria.

The return of De Gaulle

June 1958. The place is Paris. Rising above the sound of the traffic a strange, rhythmic noise can be heard. At first it is little more than a murmur. But soon it grows louder A crowd appears, marching along a wide, tree-lined avenue. In the crowd are thousands of people. As they march they chant out a slogan— Algérie Francaise, Algérie Francaise, Algérie Francaise—over and over again.

The marchers were demanding that Algeria should remain under French rule. The trouble had begun about a month earlier. A new government had been formed which seemed ready to make a deal with the Algerians. This had made many people very angry. In Algeria itself French settlers and the leaders of the army were furious. They wanted to crush the rebels, not make agreements with them. Not everyone wanted this. But one thing everyone was sure of—whatever was to be done, France needed a strong leader to do it.

French settlers and some Algerians demand that Algeria should stay French

At this moment De Gaulle announced that he was ready to take over the government of France once more. Soon the marching crowds were chanting a new slogan—De Gaulle, De Gaulle, De Gaulle. They got their wish. A few days later De Gaulle took over as Prime Minister.

But he made certain conditions. The first was that for six months he must be allowed to rule as he wanted to, without asking parliament. The second was that during this time a new constitution must be worked out.

The new constitution was soon ready. The French people were asked to vote whether they wanted it to be introduced. Most of them decided that they did. In October 1958 the Fifth Republic, which was based on the new constitution, came into being.

The new constitution gave most of the power to rule France to one man, the President. De Gaulle was elected to hold this new position. The French people gave him the power to do whatever he thought best to solve the country's problems.

An opposition poster in the vote of 1958

De Gaulle speaking from a balcony in Algiers

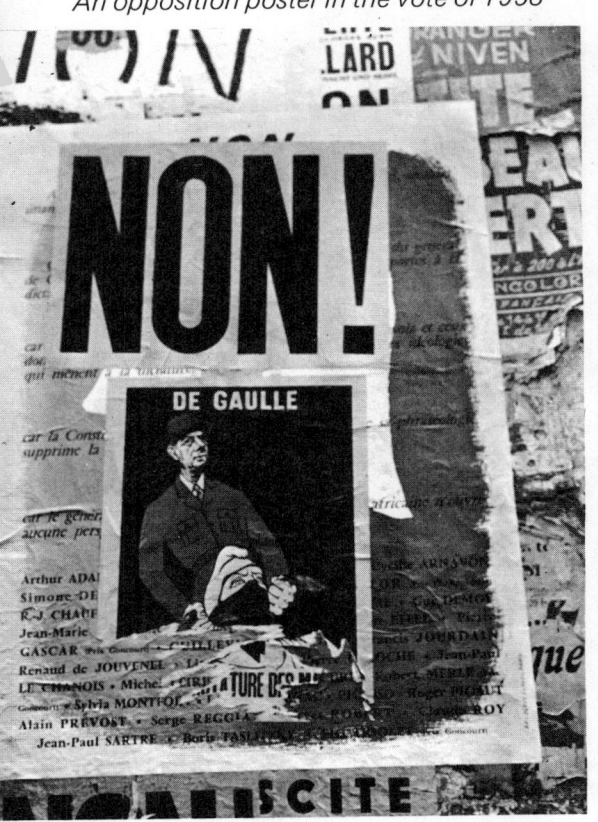

19

The rule of De Gaulle

From 1958 onwards De Gaulle gave France strong and lasting government. In 1961 he ended the long and costly war in Algeria. He did this by giving the Algerians their independence. This was a terrible shock to many of the people who had helped to bring him to power. They accused De Gaulle of betraying France and a number of generals plotted to overthrow him. When this plan failed, De Gaulle's enemies formed a secret organisation called the O.A.S. The main aim of the O.A.S. was to kill De Gaulle. But all its schemes failed and most of its members ended up in prison or fled to other countries.

De Gaulle was a proud and haughty man. He disliked the way in which the United States always expected the countries of west Europe to follow her lead in dealings with the Soviet Union. He made it clear that France was not going to follow anybody's lead. He set scientists to make an atomic bomb. This was so that France would not have to depend on the United States to defend her from an attack by nuclear bombs. He then left NATO and ordered it to close all its bases in France. De Gaulle's aim was to show the world that France was still a great and powerful nation who suited herself in her dealings with other countries.

De Gaulle gave the people of France new pride and confidence in their country. But not everyone liked his rule. Many young people thought that he

An O.A.S. bomb exploded here

was old fashioned and domineering. Many workers were dissatisfied with their wages and hours of work. In May 1968, this dissatisfaction boiled over. Thousands of students marched through the streets of Paris shouting for De Gaulle to resign. Millions of workers came out on strike.

The government sent truck loads of armed police roaring into Paris to restore order. But the students tore up paving stones and chopped down trees

A barricade in the centre of Paris

to make barricades. There was fighting in the streets. Overturned cars blazed in the night. Tear gas bit at people's eyes and nostrils. The air was filled with angry shouts and the sound of explosions. Many people feared that France was on the edge of a civil war.

The trouble took De Gaulle by surprise. But he kept his nerve and order was restored. After giving the workers higher wages and promising other changes, De Gaulle ordered a new parliament to be elected. The riots had frightened many voters, and the new parliament contained even more of De Gaulle's supporters than the old one. But he felt that people had lost confidence in him. A year later he resigned and the people of France elected Georges Pompidou as their new President.

In 1970 De Gaulle died. The men who ruled France after him were less fixed in their ideas. They showed themselves to be more ready to compromise on problems within France and in their dealings with other countries.

Towards one Europe — the Schuman Plan

To be well off a country needs thriving industries. Thriving industries need steel to build factories, dams and bridges, to make machinery, cars, trucks and ships.

Two main ingredients are used to make steel — coal and iron ore. West Europe has plenty of both. But although the main coal and iron fields are close together, they lie in different countries. This can be seen from the map. In the Saar area of Germany there are many coal mines. But the nearest iron ore is just across the border, in France. If the French iron ore and the German coal can be brought together without a lot of fuss about customs duties both

Jean Monnet* and Robert Schumann

Coal and iron deposits of west Europe

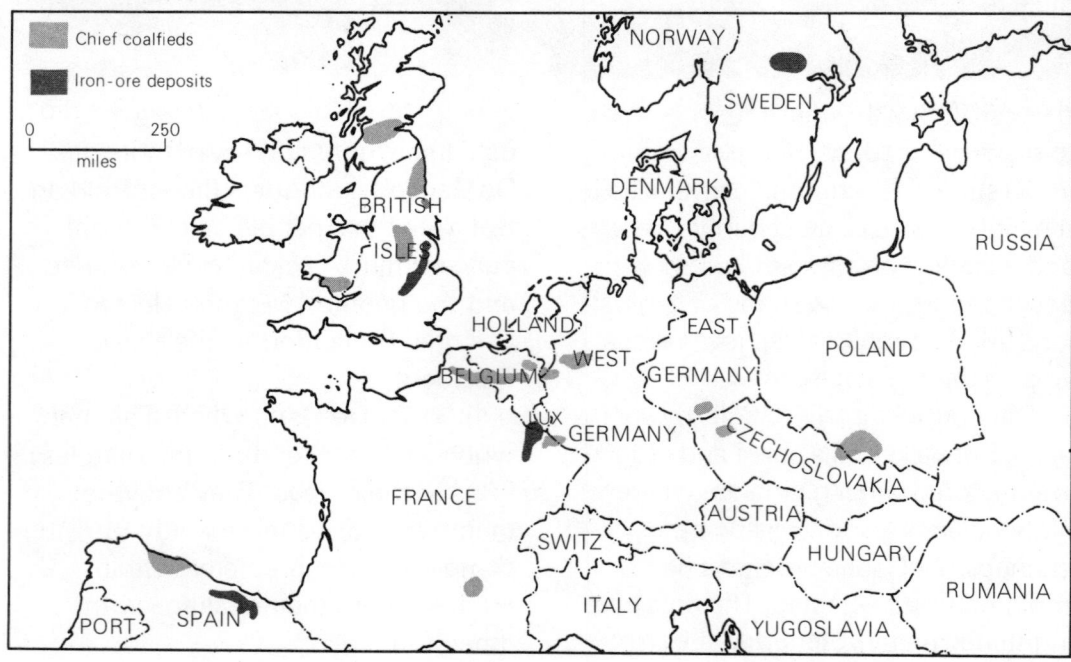

countries can benefit.

In 1950, the Foreign Minister of France, Robert Schuman, suggested a way to bring this about. His suggestion was called the Schuman Plan. But another Frenchman named Jean Monnet* was the real brain behind the scheme.

Monnet's idea was simple—so far as the coal and steel industries were concerned, why not just do away with frontiers? Then all the countries would be able to get their raw materials more easily. They would also have more customers for their coal and steel.

Monnet's plan had another advantage. The giant German steel industry had built the tanks and the bombers with which Hitler had conquered Europe. Germany's neighbours did not want this to happen again. On the other hand, they all needed German coal and steel to re-build their prosperity. How could Germany's industries be made strong again without everyone having to worry about another Hitler coming along?

The Schuman plan solved this problem. It set up an organisation called the European Coal and Steel Community. France, West Germany, Italy, Belgium, Holland and Luxemburg became members. They soon came to be known as 'the Six'. They agreed to join their separate coal and steel industries and run them as one big concern.

The scheme was run by experts from each member country. This meant that neither Germany, nor any other country in the Community, could use its in-

The first train to cross the frontier between France and Luxembourg under the Coal and Steel Community agreements

dustries in a way which the others did not like. This group of experts was called the High Authority. Its first head was Jean Monnet.

The European Coal and Steel Community went into action in 1952. It worked very well. Trade in coal and steel between the Six increased and in only three years twenty-five per cent more steel was produced every year. The Six were delighted. They quickly began to plan other ways of working together.

*Pronounced Zhon Monnay

23

The birth of the Common Market

Rome, 2,000 years ago. Drums thudding, trumpets blaring, crowds cheering. The legions are home! Another land has been conquered by their soldiers and added to the mighty Roman Empire. The legions march proudly into the city, the sun glinting on their spears and armour. Behind them stumble thousands of prisoners, driven along by guards cracking heavy cattle whips.

In ancient times, Rome was the most powerful city in the world. Nothing could stop the march of her legions—neither burning deserts, thick forests nor snow-capped mountains. The Romans ruled most of Europe as well as large parts of Asia and Africa.

Time has moved on, almost 2,000 years, to the year 1957. Once more Rome is the meeting place of men who dream of bringing all Europe together under one government. But these men are very different from the Emperors who had united the people of Europe by war; these men planned to unite them by trade.

The men who met in Rome in 1957 were the leaders of the six nations of the European Coal and Steel Community. They had come to sign an agreement to work together in other matters. The agreement was called the Treaty of Rome. This set up the European Economic Community, or the Common Market as it is often called.

In the Treaty of Rome the Six set out

Signing the Treaty of Rome, 1957

their aims. These were the three most important:

1 Removing all barriers to trade, such as customs duties, between member countries. Modern industries work best if they can produce goods in large amounts. They can only do this if they have plenty of customers— that is if they have a big market. One country may not have enough people to give its industries a big market. But several countries joined together make a very big market—in the case of the Six, a market of over 180 million people.

2 Free movement of people between one Common Market country and another. This way, if people in one

24

0   500
       miles

NORWAY   FINLAND

SWEDEN

BRITISH   DENMARK
ISLES

RUSSIA

HOLLAND
BELGIUM   EAST
LUX   GERMANY   POLAND

WEST   CZECHOSLOVAKIA
FRANCE   GERMANY

SWITZ   AUSTRIA   HUNGARY

RUMANIA

ITALY   YUGOSLAVIA

PORTUGAL   BULGARIA
SPAIN   ALBANIA

TURKEY

MOROCCO   ALGERIA

Countries of the Common Market

country were out of work they could
get jobs in another country where
work was plentiful. In later years
large numbers of Italians went to
work in German factories.

3 Building a kind of wall of customs
   duties round the Common Market:
   This was to encourage the people of
   the Six to buy goods they needed
   from one another instead of from
   outsiders. For example it would be
   cheaper for a Frenchman to buy a
   German or an Italian car then to buy
   a similar British one. The British car
   would have to have customs duties
   paid on it before it could be sold in
   France; the German and Italian cars
   would not.

Italian workers in a German factory

The Common Market in action

In 1943 Heinz Otte was a 16 year old boy soldier in Hitler's army. By the time he was 18 he had been wounded fighting the Russians and finally captured by the Americans. When the fighting ended he was homeless, hungry and without a job. Like millions of other Germans he had to set about trying to build a new life for himself.

By 1962 he had succeeded. He was earning a steady wage of almost £20 a week, fitting rear axles to Volkswagen cars. This was good money at that time.

Heinz was able to build a house for his wife and two children and to buy a new car every year.

The story of Heinz Otte is not an unusual one. By the 1960's most people in west Europe were much better off. This was especially true in the Common Market countries, such as West Germany. The diagrams show this. They show the rises in wages and in industrial output (i.e. in the number of goods being turned out by factories) in the two largest Common Market

The production line at the Volkswagon factory

countries—France and West Germany—between 1954 and 1960. After 1960 both wages and output continued to rise. Between 1960 and 1965 industrial output in the Common Market increased by almost a third—double the rise which took place in Britain. This meant that by the late 1960's the people of west Europe were better off than ever before in their history.

But many people look upon the Common Market as much more than just an arrangement to make people better off. They see it as a way to make the people of Europe think of themselves as members of one family instead of as deadly rivals.

One attempt to do this had been made in 1949, when an organisation called the Council of Europe was set up. This was a kind of Parliament to which most of the nations of west Europe sent representatives. But the Council of Europe had no powers to make laws and so it never had much influence.

Many people believe that the Common Market may succeed where the Council of Europe failed. They hope that one day it will grow into a kind of United States of Europe, with one parliament and one government for the whole continent.

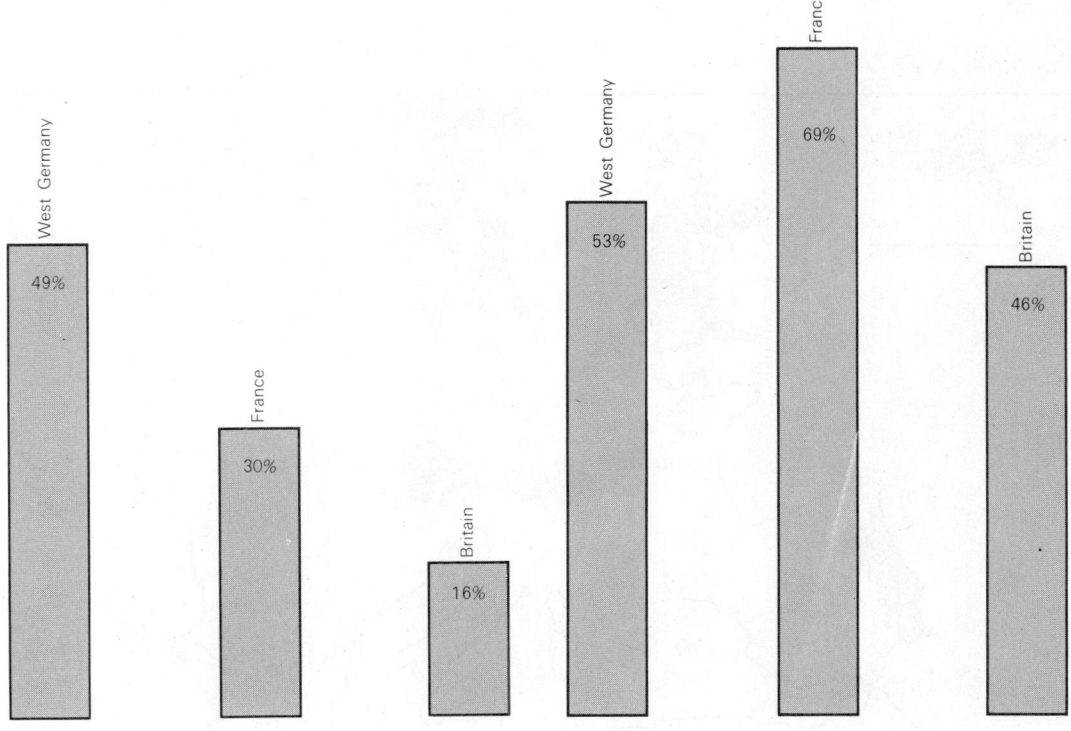

Increase in output between 1954 and 1960

Increase in wages between 1954 and 1960

West Germany 49%
France 30%
Britain 16%

West Germany 53%
France 69%
Britain 46%

Britain and the Common Market

When the Common Market was set up in 1957 Britain could easily have become a member. But she decided not to. The people of Britain did not really think of themselves as European. Britain is an island, cut off from the rest of Europe by the sea. She has close trading links with the Commonwealth—that is the various countries over which she once ruled. Some of these countries—New Zealand, Canada and Australia—have many people of British descent. If Britain joined the Common Market, the close family ties with these countries might be harmed. Joining the Common Market would mean also that Britain had to give up part of her power to run her own affairs. In 1957 she would not do this.

Instead of joining the Common Market Britain took the lead in forming the European Free Trade Association, or EFTA. This was a much looser group than the Common Market, but some of its aims were similar. EFTA set out to do away with customs duties on trade between its seven member countries. But only 90 million people live in the EFTA countries, compared with 180 million in the Common Market. Fewer people meant fewer customers and so industry and trade in the EFTA countries did not

Countries in EFTA

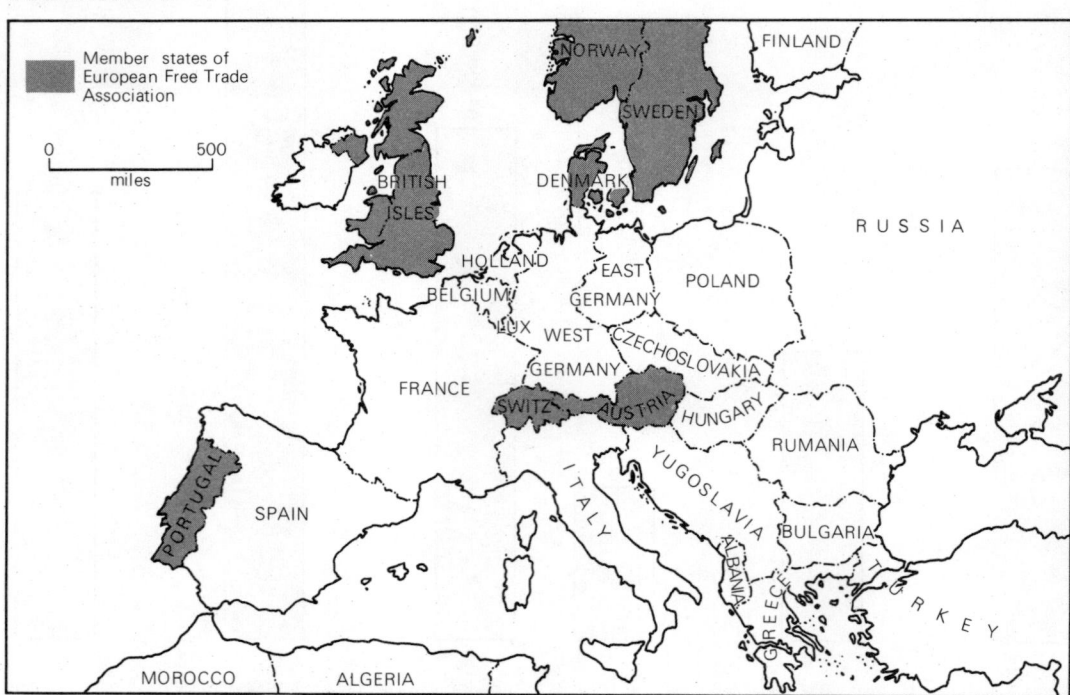

In 1967 the Labour Government tried to join the Common Market. Mr Wilson and Mr Brown with President de Gaulle

grow as fast as the Common Market.

By 1961, it was clear that if Britain was to prosper she had to sell more of her goods to the Common Market. Yet each year the Common Market countries bought more from each other. There seemed only one answer for Britain: to become a member. Not everyone was keen. Farmers, for example, feared they would get lower prices for their produce. However, the Conservative government made the first attempt to join in 1961. It failed, mainly because of President de Gaulle.

All Common Market members must agree before a new country may join. De Gaulle said that Britain would not give full loyalty to Europe because of her strong ties with the Commonwealth and the U.S.A. In 1967 the Labour government tried to join, but once more de Gaulle said 'No'. At the start of the 1970s Mr. Heath's government asked again. De Gaulle was no longer in power. This time Britain succeeded. On 1 January 1973 she became a member of the Common Market.

Towards one Europe—past, present and future

'This noble continent is the origin of most of the culture, arts, philosophy and science of both ancient and modern times. If Europe were once united in the sharing of its common inheritance, there would be no limit to the happiness, to the prosperity and glory which its three to four hundred million people would enjoy.' *Winston Churchill,* 1946.

The history of Europe is a long, blood-soaked story of wars between its nations. World War Two was the terrible climax to centuries of killing and destruction. When the war ended many people saw that if the nations of Europe wanted a worthwhile future they had to learn one very important lesson—to live in peace with one another.

This dream of a more friendly Europe got off to a bad start. In 1945, the continent was split into two by the Iron Curtain. But the outlook was not completely black. Schemes like the Schuman Plan and the Common Market showed that even old enemies like

Europe is still divided. A watchtower on the frontier between east and west Germany

Czechoslovakia 1968: young men of Bratislava stone invading Russian tanks

France and Germany could work together when they really wanted to.

But for years there was no friendship or working together between the nations of east and west Europe. The barbed wire fences of the Iron Curtain cut across the continent like a scar. The nations on each side of the Curtain lived in different worlds. They were full of fears and suspicions and had little to do with one another.

But by the start of the 1970's things were beginning to change. The nations of west Europe depended less upon the United States. Those of east Europe were no longer controlled quite so tightly by the Russians. They became less afraid of one another. Their leaders visited one another's countries. Tele-vision programmes were exchanged. Singers, actors and dancers travelled across the Iron Curtain to entertain audiences on the other side.

There were still big differences. Germany was still divided. The Berlin Wall was still standing. The forces of NATO and the Warsaw Pact kept a close watch on one another. The Russians sent tanks into Czechoslovakia. Even so at the beginning of the 1970's, the chances for a friendlier Europe seemed brighter than anyone would have dreamed possible a few years earlier. Some people even began to wonder if one day the Iron Curtain might disappear so that all the nations of Europe, east as well as west, could come together in peace and friendship.

To write

1 Imagine you are an American living in 1947. You have just heard about General Marshall's plan to help Europe. Write a letter to a newspaper either supporting or opposing the plan and giving your reasons.
2 Draw a picture diagram to show the ways in which the Marshall plan helped Europe.
3 Draw a six picture strip cartoon showing the highlights of either French or German history since 1945. Give each picture a suitable caption.
4 Imagine you are an east Berliner who wants to escape to west Berlin. Write a letter to a friend saying why and trying to persuade him to join you. Then write the friend's reply, in which he refuses to go and says why.
5 Draw a diagram called 'Towards One Europe'. On it show the various ways in which the nations of Europe have started working together more closely since 1945.
6 Write a letter to a newspaper either supporting or opposing the idea of Britain joining the Common Market. Give your reasons.
7 On an outline map of Europe mark in the Iron Curtain; the Common Market countries; the EFTA countries; Berlin; Rome; Paris.
8 Pick out the three things that have happened in west Europe since 1945 that you think were most important. Write a short paragraph about each of them.

For discussion

1 Which kind of goods was it most important for the countries of Europe to spend Marshall aid on?
2 Despite the help they gave to Europe the Americans became quite unpopular in some west European countries after World War Two. Can you think of any reasons for this?
3 Why did the Americans and the British risk a war rather than let the Russians take control of Berlin in 1948? Would they be right to do the same thing again?
4 Would it be a good thing for the rest of Europe if Germany stayed divided?
5 Was it right to re-arm the Germans?
6 Is a good military leader, like a general, likely to make a good ruler in peace time?
7 Would one government for all the countries of Europe be a good thing?
8 Should Britain join the Common Market? What would be the advantages and the disadvantages?
9 Would you object to having a foreigner as your boss at work?

To find out

1 Find out what you can about the attempts that have been made to escape from east to west Berlin across the Berlin Wall.
2 Find out what you can about each of the following people:— General Eisenhower; President Truman; Konrad Adenauer; Ludwig Erhard; Willi Brandt; Daniel Cohn Bendit; General Raoul Salan; Georges Pompidou.
3 Make a scrap book (using newspaper cuttings etc) about any one Common Market country.
4 Find out more about the man who, in your opinion, is the most important west European leader since the war.
5 Find out what you can about the following:— The Potsdam Conference; the Warsaw Pact; Comecon; The Brandenburg Gate; Bonn; Euratom; the Volkswagen Company.
6 Ask any adults you know how they would feel about having a foreigner as their boss at work.
7 Find out what differences there are between the way of life in a communist country of east Europe and a nation in West Europe.